GAME OF THRONES: AN UNOFFICIAL TRAVEL GUIDE

TABLE OF CONTENTS

ABOUT THE AUTHOR

Before you start up with "You know nothing, Paul Oswell", here's a little bit about my credentials. I've been a journalist and travel writer since 1999, writing mostly for newspapers (*The Guardian, The Daily Mail*), magazines and websites in the UK, but also some international publications and inflight magazines. I've also written multiple guide books about New Orleans (where I've lived since 2011) and published two travel books: New Orleans For Free and New Orleans Historic Hotels. I run an online travel magazine called Shandy Pockets (www.shandypockets.com) and I am, of course, a fan of GoT. Please feel free to send me feedback (paul.oswell@gmail.com) or visit my personal website at www.pauloswell.com.

ACKNOWLEDGEMENTS

Huge thanks to Julia Sevin for help with the cover design and Abby Waysdorf for permission to reprint her excellent essay. A big thanks also to John Buckingham for his permission to use his photo of the Dark Hedges for the cover.

DISCLAIMER

The information in this book is for informative purposes only. Although this book strives to provide accurate and current information, there is no guarantee (directly or indirectly) with respect to the completeness, accuracy, reliability or suitability of the information.

This book has no affiliation with and is not endorsed by Game of Thrones, HBO, or George R.R. Martin. Game of Thrones is a copyrighted show, owned by HBO.

All photos, videos, audio, and quotes are copyright to their respective owners and no copyright infringement is intended. If you claim copyright to any item or items displayed in this book and wish to have them removed please contact me at paul.oswell@gmail.com and they will be removed immediately without question.

All maps are presented for illustrative purposes only. They were created with MapBox, an open source software programme that enables users to create royalty-free maps. Go to www.mapbox.com for more information.

INTRODUCTION

As a new fantasy drama burst into our screens in 2011, it was hard to imagine – even for those that had read George R R Martin's books – what kind of a world we'd all become immediately transfixed by.

For newcomers to the GoT world especially, those first glimpses of Winterfell and King's Landing were tantalising. The gradual expansion into the world we know over five seasons has been visually breathtaking – all the more so for knowing that not everything has been CGI'd on a huge sound stage, but that parts of our world have been skilfully woven into this modern legend.

There are many elements that contribute to the success of the TV show. The superb casting, the adaptations of the plots for television and the special effects are all part of it. Another huge factor of the show's success, though, is the range of stunning backdrops that the location teams continue to choose, and that the photographers continue to capture.

Martin's books have used actual historical events as the broad basis of some of their plot lines, so it seems fitting that the show would use some of the world's most incredible scenery and architecture as visual inspiration for both the actors' performances and for fanatical viewers at home.

The fictional continents of Westeros and Essos – from the frozen wastelands beyond the wall to the sun-blasted landscapes of Slaver's Bay – are brought to life by the panoramas of some of Europe's most evocative locations. Country roads in Northern Ireland, glaciers in Iceland and ancient arenas in Spain have all graced our screens in their full beauty.

The really beautiful thing, though? The fact that you can visit these places. That's what this book is for. I've tried to give you as much information as I can via my experience as a travel writer so that you can make the most of your experience as a traveller and GoT fan. I don't know where you're coming from, so you'll have to work out the initial flight or drive for yourself, but once you get to Dubrovnik or Belfast or Reykjavik, this guide will hopefully be of use.

As well as maps and lists of the actual locations used in the TV show, I've listed appropriate places to stay, general travel tips and some suggestions for things to see that aren't necessarily connected with GoT.

I hope you enjoy the book and, even if you don't have any trips planned, that it gives you a sense of these cities and towns and beaches and parks. I've enjoyed putting it together.

Safe travels to you.

Paul Oswell

New Orleans, July 2015

P.S. I was originally going to include the United States, just in case fans were interested in visiting the places that George R R Martin grew up around. There wasn't enough to really merit a chapter, but he grew up in Bayonne, New Jersey and went to Mary Jane Donohoe School and Marist High School. I'm sure that if you're a GoT superfan, these are already on your list.

Who Does GoT Tourism and Why?

By Abby Waysdorf

Fort Lovrijenac looks the part, a stone fortress looming over the sparkling blue water of the sea framing Dubrovnik. It has thick, stone walls, small windows, the city motto carved over the entrance. Within, it's easy to recognize the spot where Cersei confronted Littlefinger, even without the draped fabric and potted plants. Standing there, on top of the aged white stones, everything seems strangely close.

Of course, in other ways, Lovrijenac doesn't feel right at all–it's small and empty, and much more stark and squat than the section of the Red Keep it's supposed to portray. Gone is the tall tower, the decorations, and of course, the rest of the royal castle itself–Fort Lovrijenac, while solid, is a small fort, designed to hold mercenaries and their equipment rather than a king and his court. Still, though, it feels real.

It's experiencing that sense of "realness" that brings people to visit filming locations....

I've been researching film location tourism, and specifically Game of Thrones tourism, for the past year as part of my PhD research, including by interviewing dozens of fans. What I've seen is that the screen can only give us so much: we see the place, but we don't feel the ground or smell the air or any of the other little things that make up a full experience. It's only partial, as attached as we get to the places we see on screen and what happens there.

What this "realness" entails, though, varies a lot from person to person. Everyone I've interviewed for my research wants to see what they saw on TV, and make sure that it's the correct tree or doorway they're standing by. But the other things they want out of the location visit changes depending on what it is they like in Game of Thrones to begin with.

Fort Lovrijenac, for example, is an exciting visit for the Game of Thrones tourist not just because parts of it are easily recognizable, but because it also has a sense of history. Clearly medieval, there's a heft and solidity to it that immediately marks it as something more than a "typical set" of wood and painted cloth.

If you're the kind of Game of Thrones fan who likes how much it feels like actual medieval history, seeing that reflected in the medieval structures that the show films is appealing.

The built sets are off-limits, so much of what the visitor gets is historic structures – castles and ruined abbeys, towers and city walls. Many of the people I interviewed loved the historical aspect of the show. Being in a historical space, learning about the "real story" behind what Game of Thrones used, enhanced this feeling that the show was reflecting the past. There's an insider appeal to this kind of knowledge, knowing what "really happened" where the show took place, which allow for a connection with history. Game of Thrones provides a frame for understanding what went on here centuries ago, a way to bring the past of these locations into focus and make it vibrant and real.

There's also the "realness" of what happened there much more recently, the difference between what we see on screen and what we see when we visit. Discovering what the production staff did, be they the scouts and set designers or the editors and CGI programmers, is intriguing. Stories about what really went on during filming, imagining what it must have taken to find the location and how they transported the equipment, feeling the heat or cold and realizing what the actors may have been through, all of it shades in Game of Thrones. Some are lucky enough to catch glimpses of filming, or they're there in enough time that there are still relics of it about, adding to the sense that they were really where things happened and can figure out how it happened.

And then there's imaginative play in general–imagining what King's Landing or Winterfell could be like, reenacting scenes and saying lines. It's fun to play with some of the boundaries between reality and fantasy. Not that anyone really believed that they were 'in Westeros', of course, but they enjoyed playing with the idea that they could be, by moving and feeling and sensing the environment. Being in those spaces fills in the fan's sense of what Westeros and Essos are, what they might look like beyond the bits seen on TV and what the weather might be like if you went there.

Whatever "real" means, being there is a unique and personal experience. People find it hard to put into words, because it's not really something that can be expressed that way. It's all about feeling the place, about making a personal connection to Game of Thrones. Yes, it can be shared on Facebook and talked about to your friends, but that's not the same as being there. That belongs to the person who went, and them alone.

And who are the Game of Thrones tourists? That was one of the more fascinating aspects of my research. I talked to teenage boys and 60-something women, committed fantasy geeks and Harvard Business School students on yacht week. It was a portrait of the kind of audience Game of Thrones captures. It can be assumed that the show attracts a variety of viewers based on the ratings, but seeing them all brings the point home. This is something that has resonated with a lot of people, and many who would have never thought about fantasy before. Yet here they were.

For many (although certainly not all) of these fans, visiting the locations was also the only sort of fan activity they did. While the Internet makes it easier and easier for fans to read about and discuss their object of fandom with others, and the idea of doing so is fairly commonplace, it's worth remembering that not everyone wants to do this. The fans I talked to who didn't had various reasons. Some, while they enjoy the show, still think that spending time discussing it online is a geek line they don't want to cross. Others feel that the fandom won't be welcoming to them–that participation is reserved for those who are experts, or at least with the very strong opinion that they are, and they'll be rejected. A few were afraid of spoilers (although as an aside, I've found the Game of Thrones community is very good about hiding them). Others just said they didn't have time.

Visiting filming locations bypasses all of this. You're already on vacation, so you don't need to take time out of a busy work schedule to post or think about posting. They can also fit into other vacation plans, whether it's a cruise stopping in Dubrovnik for a day or a family heritage trip to Northern Ireland. It's also something that can be scaled to different levels of fandom.

When I was doing my fieldwork last year, most of the sites were found by a quick Google search, or by paying for the new tours that were running, and since then it's only become easier to find and get to the locations.

Castle Ward, site of Winterfell, is advertising "Game of Thrones experiences," the Dubrovnik tourist board offers a Game of Thrones map on its website, and more tours are available at both locations. Once there, there are no gatekeepers judging knowledge of the show, and the locations are the same whether you've just finished binge-watching Season One or have been in since the pilot. And if you are a more adventurous fan, there are always more obscure locations to find.

And there's an allure to location visiting. Big spreads have run in The New York Times, The Guardian, and a range of other newspapers, talking about how great it is to go. Government ministers have shown up. It's not coded as something overly "geeky"—just lightly so, just enough to be fun, essentially sightseeing with a twist. And the appeal of "being there" is strong throughout popular culture, despite/because of the ability to virtually "be" anywhere. It's "better" to be at a concert rather than watching it on DVD, for example, and this extends to the idea of being at the filming location.

There's something that's just cool about actually being there. And in doing so, it becomes real, becomes your own. That's something that transcends fan type.

Reproduced by kind permission of Abby Waysdorf. Abby is a Simpsons fan transplanted to the Low Countries. She's also a PhD candidate at Erasmus University Rotterdam, where her study focuses on film and television-inspired tourism. You can learn more about her research at locatingimagination.com, or follow her on Twitter at @awfully_good.

LOCATIONS

(AS OF THE END OF SEASON FIVE)

CROATIA

ICELAND

MALTA

MOROCCO

NORTHERN IRELAND

SCOTLAND

SPAIN

CROATIA

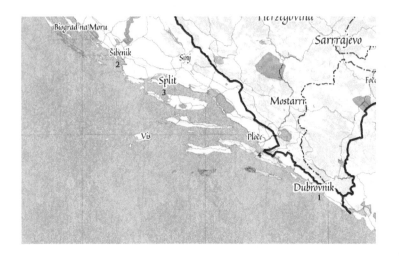

The Mediterranean climate, glistening blue waters and medieval walled fortifications of Croatia must have been an instant hit with the GoT location scouts. It's hard to argue with the choice. The fascinating mix of historic architectural styles – everything from palazzos to fortresses to Roman columns – is a perfect storm of dazzling backdrops, and the sun reflecting off the idyllic coastline makes it an even more inspired choice. GoT began filming in Croatia in Season Two as the scope of operations expanded, and King's Landing took shape amid the scenic ancient city of Dubrovnik. Other Croatian locations were gradually added and were given that GoT magic to film scenes that took place in the fictional environs of Qarth, Meereen, Braavos and Slaver's Bay.

> "THE MORNING AIR WAS THICK WITH THE OLD FAMILIAR STINKS OF KING'S LANDING. (CERSEI LANNISTER) BREATHED IN THE SCENTS OF SOUR WINE, BREAD BAKING, ROTTING FISH AND NIGHTSOIL, SMOKE AND SWEAT AND HORSE PISS. NO FLOWER HAD EVER SMELLED SO SWEET."

1. Dubrovnik

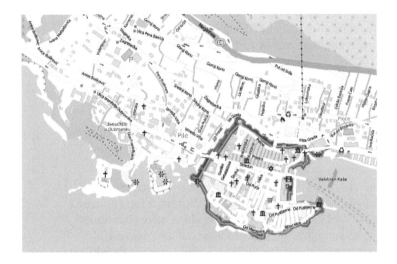

Long before GoT showcased its visual delights, the architecture and coastal views to be found around this incredible city had already been inspiring poets, artists and visitors alike for centuries.

The mighty defensive walls that you see today were erected in the 15th century (though some parts date back to the 9th century) and there are ancient monuments and buildings enough for it to have been made a UNESCO World Heritage Site in 1979.

Set on a peninsula and surrounded by dramatic cliffs, the sun bounces off the white walls of the city and onto the atmospheric, sun-soaked port. King's Landing couldn't really be more well-illustrated in real life than by this gem of the Adriatic Sea. You can almost believe it's the capital of the Seven Kingdoms and the seat of the Iron Throne.

This was confirmed by showrunners David Benioff and D.B. Weiss in an interview for HBO:

"King's Landing might be the single most important location in the entire show, and it has to look right," they said. "To find a full-on, immaculately preserved medieval walled city that actually looks uncannily like King's Landing where the bulk of our show is set, that was in and of itself such an amazing find."

"IF YOU HAVE A GOOD NOSE YOU CAN SMELL THE TREACHERY TOO."

JAIME LANNISTER

Tip: The very best time to visit Dubrovnik is between September and October. At this time, the temperatures aren't stifling hot and yet most of the cruise ships have abandoned the port, so you have the place to yourself a bit more. Hotel prices are pretty steep during May-August, but wait a while for the hordes to leave town and jump in during this short window.

Getting there: Croatia Airlines is the national airline, and though its main hub is in Zagreb, it has flights from many European cities to Dubrovnik. See www.croatiaairlines.com for more details. Dubrovnik Airport is located in Cilipi and is about 18 km (12 miles) outside the city. There are plenty of bus and taxi services.

Stay: For the full GoT experience, stay in the same hotel that the cast and crew stayed in while they were filming here – The Hotel Excelsior Dubrovnik (www.adriaticluxuryhotels.com) – which is over 100 years old. The Pucic Palace (www.thepucicpalace.com) is another suitably regal option, while Hotel Kazbek (www.kazekdubrovnik.com) is a great-value 16th century stone villa.

See also: Dubrovnik Cathedral, the Dubrovnik Cable Car, The Franciscan Monastery, War Photo Limited Museum, Rector's Palace (The Dubrovnik Museum).

Tourist information: www.tzdubrovnik.hr/eng/

CITY WALLS

VIEW OF THE OLD WALLS (IMAGE VIA CREATIVE COMMONS LICENSE, MORGUEFILE)

During the summer season, you can stroll across the incredible city walls any time between 9am and 6.30pm. There's a nominal entrance fee, but it's well worth the price. Looking out across the bay you don't have to have too much imagination to conjure up images of the Battle of Blackwater Bay. You can see Lovrjenac Fortress (see below) just across the gleaming waters, an ancient fortification which was transformed for GoT into the majestic Red Fort.

> "COME WITH ME AND TAKE THIS CITY!"
>
> STANNIS BARATHEON, THE BATTLE OF BLACKWATER BAY

The highlight for GoT fans is definitely the Minčeta Tower, which looms up at the walls' highest point and stands as a potent symbol of how impenetrable the city was. This tower portrayed the infamous House of the Undying, where Daenerys Targaryan had some surreal encounters (admittedly many of her experiences are) and set about rescuing her dragons.

The fort – which dates back to the 14th century – is topped with a stone Gothic crown that instils a palpable sense of power.

There are three entrances to the walls: near the Pile Gate, the Ploče Gate and at the Maritime Museum. The Pile Gate entrance is the most popular, but entering from the Ploče Gate does mean that you can get some of the steepest climbs out of the way first.

Tip: It's a more demanding walk than you might think, so try and do it early in the morning or later in the afternoon, and take plenty of water as there are few vendors and they tend to be overpriced.

(IMAGE VIA CREATIVE COMMONS LICENSE, COURTESY OF DANIEL ORTMANN)

GRADAC PARK

GRADAC PARK (IMAGE VIA CREATIVE COMMONS LICENSE, COURTESY OF KIGSZ)

This lesser-known (until now, perhaps) park sits around 200m from the Old Town, and climbing the steps leading up to it gives you a view over the roofs of the ancient houses. It has charming tree-lined pathways, ponds and fountains. The perfect spot, then, for a royal wedding reception, and this is where the ill-fated Purple Wedding of King Joffrey and Margaery Tyrell took place.

> "MY OWN WEDDING IS LOOKING MUCH BETTER IN HINDSIGHT."
>
> TYRION LANNISTER MEDITATES ON THE OUTCOMES OF THE PURPLE AND RED WEDDINGS

Game of Thrones writer Cat Taylor spoke about the wedding in her online production diary, revealing some of the details.

"While the ceremony itself was filmed in one of our semi-permanent sets in Belfast, the Sept of Baelor, the reception was filmed in a beautiful outdoor set located in Park Gradac in Dubrovnik, Croatia. The park was transformed by our new Production Designer, Deb Riley, and her team into everything you might desire from a Royal Wedding carnival, with elaborate decorations, an epic feast and the most creative and unexpected forms of entertainment for the guests.

Filmed over a five-day stretch, we waited with bated breath each day for the clouds to roll in and dampen our fun. Weather reports suggested imminent downpours at the end of the week, and only a few days before, water funnels had formed off the coast in the height of a rainstorm. Aside from one short and dramatic burst where Costume scrambled to get all the extras under cover and everyone rushed to protect props, we were spared the worst of the predictions.

In terms of principal cast members in attendance, the Royal Wedding was one of the largest scenes we've filmed since the premiere season, with 23 named parts appearing on any given day. In addition, we were delighted to welcome 218 extras as guests to the event, some of them travelling from the other side of Europe and the United States to be a part of the experience. Lookout for some familiar faces in the crowds – Pixie Le Knot is back this year, and one of our crew makes an appearance with the entertainers."(via www.blastr.com)

LOKRUM ISLAND

It's just a ten-minute ferry ride to this beautiful island, where scenes set in Qarth, the 'Queen of Cities', were filmed. The landscape drifts between lush forests and rocky beaches, and people come for a day trip to picnic and go swimming. Legend has it that the island was cursed by monks, foretelling great misfortune to anyone that would buy land there.

Some memorable scenes were filmed here, such as the welcome party thrown by Xaro. It's also where the House of the Undying is set in the GoT world, and some of Daenerys' weird, magical experiences were set here.

> "BLOOD OF MY BLOOD...THIS IS AN EVIL PLACE, A HAUNT OF GHOSTS AND MAEGI. SEE HOW IT DRINKS THE MORNING SUN? LET US GO BEFORE IT DRINKS US AS WELL."
>
> JHOGO, TO DAENERYS TARGARYEN

Getting there: Catch the ferry at the Old Harbour – they usually run hourly though this increases to half-hourly in the summer.

Lovrijenac Fortress (The Fort of Saint Lawrence)

Općina Dubrovnik

Lovijenac Fortress stands proudly atop a 37m-high rock and fans will immediately recognise it as The Red Keep. Some historians date some parts of the fort back to the 11th century, though most of it was built ion the early 14th century. Still not exactly a modern structure. Over the entrance, an ancient inscription reads as follows: NON BENE PRO TOTO LIBERTAS VENDITUR AURO. This translates as 'Freedom is not sold for all the gold in the world', a saying which many GoT characters could probably relate to. You can visit the fort as part of your city walls walking tour – there isn't much to see inside apart from the stone walls, but the views back across the city are well worth the walk up.

> "The Red Keep shelters two sorts of people, Lord Eddard," Varys said. "Those who are loyal to the realm, and those who are loyal only to themselves."

Trsteno Gardens

POTOK 20, TRSTENO, +385 (0)20 751 019,
WWW.DUBROVNIKSUNGARDENS.COM

NEPTUNE STATUE, TRSTENO GARDENS (IMAGE VIA
CREATIVE COMMONS LICENSE)

14km from the centre of Dubrovnik, you'll find the
breathtaking Renaissance-style arboretum at Trsteno Gardens.

The garden is made up of landscaped, geometric shapes lined
with colourful and scented plants and bushes, and there's also
a maze and a tranquil pond. Look for the giant plane trees that
frame Trsteno Village – they are 150 feet high and 500 years
old.

The gardens were originally the 15th century summer
residence of Gučetić-Gozze family, and its gardens have been
cultivated from the 15th century to the present day. Trsteno
has a good claim to having the oldest arboretum in Europe, and
it is certainly the only one on the Croatian Adriatic coast.

The gardens now belong to the Croatian Academy of Arts and
Sciences, but thankfully, anyone can visit to drink in the
canopies, secluded paths and tranquil promenades.

These lush surroundings are where Sansa Stark spent some of her less relentlessly miserable times at King's Landing in Season Two. There are several scenes of her chatting regally with (for which read, being manipulated by) Lady and Margaery Tyrell and living the relatively calm life of a lady of the court.

This is also the place where Varys and Tyrion trade some of their traditional friendly barbs and gossip. Their exchanges are always so wonderfully scripted, as are those between Varys and Lady Olenna Tyrell:

LORD VARYS: YOU'VE TAKEN AN INTEREST IN SANSA STARK.

LADY OLENNA TYRELL: HAVE I? BECAUSE I SPOKE TO HER ONCE IN THIS GARDEN, AND ONE OF YOUR LITTLE SPIES CAME RUNNING TO TELL YOU? WHY SHOULDN'T I TAKE AN INTEREST? SHE'S AN INTERESTING GIRL.

LORD VARYS: IS SHE?

LADY OLENNA TYRELL: NO, NOT PARTICULARLY. BUT SHE'S HAD AN INTERESTING CHILDHOOD.

Getting there: Even if you're not renting a car, you have plenty of easy options to get to Trsteno, and you can catch any of the local busses numbered 12, 15, 22 or 35 from Dubrovnik's central bus station.

Tip: There is a nominal entrance fee, and the opening hours are 7am–7pm (May-October) and 8am-4pm (November-April).

2. ŠIBENIK

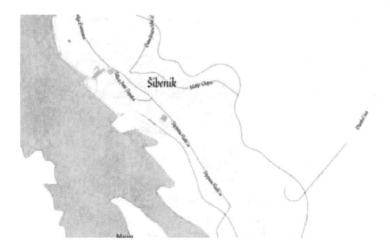

Šibenik is protected by four fortresses on each side of its medieval walls: the Fortress of St. Nicholas, St. Michael, St. John and the Šubićevac Fortress, all UNESCO protected sites. The cathedral is one of the main tourist sites, but just wandering around and taking in the Renaissance architecture really gives you a feel for the place.

This little-known medieval town makes its GoT appearance in the fifth season as the setting for Braavos, one of the Free Cities across the narrow sea. In GoT world, the city is inhabited by sailors, traders and adventurers.

The city is famously home to the imposing Iron Bank, and the many narrow streets are the backdrop to the season's adventures of Ayra Stark as she navigates her various trials and tribulations with the Many Faced Gods in the House of Black and White.

"ONE STONE CRUMBLES AND ANOTHER
TAKES ITS PLACE AND THE TEMPLE HOLDS
ITS FORM FOR A THOUSAND YEARS OR
MORE. AND THAT'S WHAT THE IRON BANK
IS, A TEMPLE. WE ALL LIVE IN ITS SHADOW
AND ALMOST NONE OF US KNOW IT. YOU
CAN'T RUN FROM THEM, YOU CAN'T CHEAT
THEM, YOU CAN'T SWAY THEM WITH
EXCUSES. IF YOU OWE THEM MONEY AND
YOU DON'T WANT TO CRUMBLE YOURSELF,
YOU PAY IT BACK."

TYWIN LANNISTER

Getting there: It's probably best to rent a car to get here,
though there are bus services from Dubrovnik bus station. The
journey takes around 6 hours, though. From the capital, you'll
take the D8 north along the coast to Ploce, then the A1, past
Split (though Split has GoT locations as well, so you could stop
here on the way). It should take just over three hours.

From Split Airport, take a bus from outside the terminal
building to the main bus station in Split. Buses are scheduled to
depart shortly after flight arrivals. From Split Bus Station, you
can take one of the numerous buses to Sibenik. The journey
time is about 1 hour 40 minutes.

Stay: Hotel accommodation isn't particularly great in Šibenik.
There are some basic hostels, and a couple of two-star
properties such as the Jadran Hotel (www.rivijera.hr) or you
can stay in more resort-style places a few minutes' drive away,
such as the much nicer Solaris Hotel
(www.solarishotelsresort.com).

See: Cathedral of St James, Memorial to Juraj Dalmatinac,
Loggia, Church of St Barbara, Church of St Nicholas

Tourism office: www.sibenik-tourism.hr

Cathedral of St James

One of the most important sights in Sibenik is the Cathedral of St. James (Katedrala sv. Jakova), and a worthy addition to the UNESCO World Heritage list. The cathedral was built between 1431 and 1536 from limestone and marble. GoT fans will recognise it as the frontage for the Iron Bank.

Krka National Park
WWW.NPKRKA.HR

This verdant nature reserve was used intermittently as general landscapes of the West, and its bright blue waterfalls are a spectacular draw. There are tranquil walks to be had along the 75km stretch of the Krka River.

Getting there: The two most popular starting points closest to Šibenik are Skradin and Lozovac at the southern end of the park. It's around a 15 minute drive from Šibenik to Lozovac, travelling north on road D33.

3. SPLIT

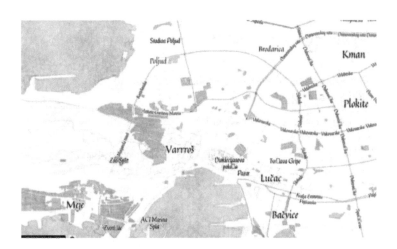

In Season Four, filming spread even further and moved north of Dubrovnik to the coastal city of Split.

Split is a lively, exuberant city that's somewhat overlooked by many tourists but offers just as fascinating a slice of Dalmatian life as its domestic rivals.

The old Riva (seafront) has recently undergone a fantastic renovation and it's a coastal hub as hip young daytrippers catch ferries to the surrounding islands.

The main locations used here were Diocletian's Palace, which is in the city centre, and then Klis Fortress and a quarry in Žrnovnica, both just outside the actual city itself.

These were the locations for much of Daenerys' struggles in Season Four, some of them memorably violent, as she fought with her new army of the Unsullied for ultimate control of the city of Meereen against the slave-owning overlords.

Getting there: From the capital, you'll take the D8 north along the coast to Ploce, then the A1 and follow signs for Split. It should take around an hour. There are private bus services from Gruz just outside Dubrovnik – some services pass through Bosnia Herzegovina, so be sure to ask about that and remember to have your passport handy if that's going to be the case.

Split also has a busy and well-served international airport, with dozens of European routes.

Stay: There are some suitably regal hotel options, including Hotel Vestibul Palace (www.vestibulpalace.com) and Hotel Peristil (www.hotelperestil.com), which are both within the palace walls. Hotel rates soar during the summer months, so consider the cheaper windows during late spring and early autumn.

Good quality/value budget accommodation has recently become more available in Split, but this portfolio is mainly made of hostels, so make sure you're comfortable with this. Private accommodation is generally a good option, especially in the summer months. If you arrive by bus, you'll be swamped at the station by women offering rooms. If you're going to take them up on the offer, be very sure that you are clear about the exact location of the room or you may find yourself several bus rides from the town centre.

See: Cathedral of St Domnius, Mestrovic Gallery, the Synagogue, Aquarium, Gallery of Fine Arts, Ethnographic Museum, Archaeological Museum, Temple of Jupiter, Golden Gate.

Tourism office: www.visitsplit.com

Diocletion's Palace

WWW.DIOCLETIANSPALACE.ORG

Although many places have a claim, this incredible structure really is one of the most impressive Roman ruins in the world. Built in AD 295 as a retirement palace for the Roman emperor Diocletian, it's a living museum right in the heart of the city - bars, shops and restaurants are all lined up inside its ancient walls.

Within these walls, you can find a myriad of street locations used for King's Landing and Meereen, as well as Daenerys' throne room. Daenerys also fought the slave-owner overlords the Mereen and Yunkai with her faithful Unsullied within these very walls, only to return to Westeros as the victorious queen.

> "You will not make Meereen rich and fat and peaceful. You will only bring it to destruction, as you did Astapor."
>
> Xaro Xhoan Daxos, to Daenerys Targaryen

Klis Fortress

This medieval fortress overlooks a village of the same name around 13km from Spilt. It isn't really on screen for very long, but it's where Daenerys plans her return to power, and even if you're not an obsessive fan, the castle and fortifications are still worth a trip out to see. The fortress offers great views across the region and parts of it date back to the 7th century.

Getting there: There are three bus lines to Klis from central Split: number 22 leaving from the National Theatre bus station and numbers 35 and 36 leaving from the bus station at Sukoisanska.

4. STON

This ancient salt-producing town (50km north west of Dubrovnik) used to be part of the Republic of Dubrovnik and it was considered so important at one point that it has five kilometres of fortifications (with 40 towers and five forts) built around it and which stand to this day. They date back to the early 14th century and it is rightly known as 'The Great Wall of Europe'.

The walls have been used as general backdrops to scenes set in King's Landing, and it's a popular day trip for GoT fans.

Getting there: There are four daily buses from Dubrovnik bus station, and it takes around 90 minutes each way.

TAKE A GOT TOUR: CROATIA

In Dubrovnik, Viator offer a 3-hour walking tour taking in King's Landing while exploring Dubrovnik's UNESCO-listed Old Town. You will also visit Lovrijenac Fortress, which witnessed some of the exploits of King Joffrey and the heroic footsteps of Ayra Stark. You can upgrade to include a 1.5-hour trip to Trsteno Arboretum to explore the historical gardens, which were used as the King's Landing palace gardens in the third season. More info: http://bit.ly/MRS5Ch

Game of Thrones Tour Croatia offer a day-long tour of Split. You'll see the 1700-year-old Diocletian's Palace and Klis Fortress, before the day ends with a traditional Croatian barbecue beside the Zrnovica River at a 600-year-old water mill, also a GoT filming location. More information: www.gameofthronestourcroatia.com

For US travellers, Zicasso have curated a week-long tour that includes all of the above, plus lessons in falconry. More info: http://www.businessinsider.com/game-of-thrones-tour-of-croatia-2014-4

ICELAND

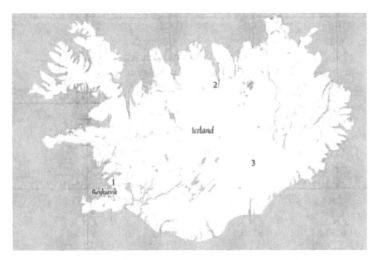

A country built on the legends of an ancient warrior race, a stark, otherworldly landscape sitting atop volcanoes and steaming geysers and a population that widely believes in the existence of elves (please, no Tyrion jokes). It's little wonder that Iceland is an ideal fit for the GoT universe.

Magical, violent but majestic nature, mythical adventure and a character that's unlike almost anywhere else on Earth. Iceland is one of a kind - that's why it offers so much and why the GoT cast and crew have managed to find so many rewarding ways to use its plentiful scenic resources. The wildest, most remote northern reaches of Westeros come to life here, including adventures north of the Wall, so chances are if you're playing a Wilding or a member of the Night's Watch, you've spent a fair amount of time wandering the Icelandic countryside. Luckily, it's a little more forgiving than the books or TV show would suggest.

In an interview for HBO, showrunner David Benioff said, "We always knew we wanted something shatteringly beautiful and barren and brutal for this part of Jon's journey, because he's in the true North now. It's all real. It's all in camera. We're not doing anything in postproduction to add mountains or snow or anything."

1. REYKJAVIK

Iceland's capital city isn't a filming location in GoT, but it's obviously the main travel hub and the place you'll probably want to use as a base to explore the rest of the country. It's also fairly close to Thingvellir National Park, which was used as a location in Season Four (see below). Take a day or two to decompress and see the sights of this weird and wonderful destination. You can easily start to get into the medieval mood with a visit to the Saga Museum, which has a tale about an ancient war boat that's about as GoT as it gets. The sites of the Reykjavik City Museum also have some fascinating Viking artefacts and history to discover. Iceland is small, and relatively easy to explore. It's not GoT related at all, nor even medieval, but you should really spend a half day taking a tour to the fluorescent pools of The Blue Lagoon, one of the most surreal places in the world. It's like swimming on the moon.

Tip: Peak season runs from June to mid-August. Good weather is fairly essential if you want to get the most out of your stay, especially for the more remote spots.

Getting there: The national carrier, Iceland Air (www.icelandair.us) has great value flights between Iceland and the US as well as Europe. It's actually a perfect stopover for US fans travelling on to explore mainland Europe.

Stay: If you can find accommodation that's not been completely booked out by the GoT cast and crew, there are some cool spots to stay in the capital, and it is much less expensive than it used to be. The Radisson Blu 1919 (www.radissonblu.com) is a fashionable boutique hotel that's in a very central location, and the Hotel Borg (www.hotelborg.is) has a lovely retro feel to it. For budget travel, there are lots of clean, modern hostels and a good choice of mid-range guest houses (*gistiheimili*).

See: The Saga Museum, the strikingly-designed Hallgrimskirkja Cathedral, the National Museum of Iceland, Reykjavik 871±2 (Viking exhibits), Vikin Maritime Museum.

Tourism office: www.visitreykjavik.is

Thingvellir National Park

This park, 45km north east of Reykjavik, is a UNESCO World Heritage Site where the Alþingi (the national parliament of Iceland) was formed in 930. It was actually based there until 1798, before being moved to Reykjavik.

The park was used as a location for the first time in Season Four, largely as the region through which Arya's and Sandor Clegane (The Hound) journeyed as they went from village to village in mid-Westeros.

> Arya Stark: When am I going to get a horse of my own?

> Sandor 'The Hound' Clegane: Little lady wants a pony.

> Arya Stark: Little lady wants away from your stench.

Getting there: The easiest way to visit is to book a tour through your hotel or a local tourism office. It's a popular spot, so you'll have plenty of choices. If you're hiring a car and driving yourself, take road no. 1 heading north out of Reykjavik. After driving through the town Mosfellsbær take the first exit to the right at roundabout onto road no. 36 to Thingvellir.

2. AKUREYRI

With less than 20,000 residents, it seems strange to refer to this as Iceland's second city, but that's exactly what it is. Just because it's rural, though, doesn't mean it doesn't have its fair share of coffee shops, cafes and nightlife, so you'll be entertained for a few days at least.

Akureyri topped Lonely Planet´s list of ten best places to visit in Europe 2015. Lonely Planet's review says among other things that Akureyri is "an easy-going place and a great base for exploring the north's green pastures, fishing villages, mudpots, waterfalls, ski fields and whale-filled bays."

The best feature for GoT fans is its proximity to several famous on-screen locations – especially if you're a fan of the Wildings and the love affair that captured viewers' hearts between Jon Snow and Ygritte.

> JON SNOW: YGRITTE, YOU WON'T WIN. I KNOW YOUR PEOPLE ARE BRAVE, NO ONE DENIES THAT.
>
> YGRITTE: YOU KNOW NOTHING, JON.

Getting there: There are daily domestic flights from Reyjavik, or you can take an all-terrain bus through the interior of the island, quite an adventure in itself. If you're driving, you'll probably want to take the coastal road (Rte 1).

Stay: The cutest property is probably the very Nordic-looking Hotel Akureyri (www.hotelakureyri.is), though the Hotel Kea (www.keahotels.is) has some nice views of the imposing, Gothic-style church.

See: The Akureyri church, Gásir Medival Trading Place, Grimsey Island, statues of Helgi the Lean and Thorunn Hyrna, Hrísey Island (the Pearl of Eyjafjörður).

Tourism office: www.visitakureyri.is

Dimmuborgir

How often do you get to wander around a twisted, criss-crossing, 2000-year old lava flow? Right, that's what we thought. As lava poured into a fiery lake (a shame all of this wasn't caught on film), a huge domed roof formed and then collapsed, leaving the incredible crags and pillars that you see today. You can explore easily thanks to a number of non-demanding, colour-coded walks and there's even a café-souvenir shop at the tip of the ridge.

If you want to stay a night in one of the world's more unusual landscapes, there's even a guesthouse. Rest assured, the accommodations are the picture of comfort and civility compared to the camp that Mance Rayder set up here.

> "WE'RE NOT IN THE SEVEN KINGDOMS, AND YOU'RE NOT DRESSED FOR THIS WEATHER."
>
> MANCE RAYDER, TO STANNIS BARATHEON

Besides, the translation of Dimmuborgir means 'Dark Castle', so, you know…how can you not want to go? One word of warning, though. According to Icelandic folklore, Dimmuborgir is connected to hell, and added to this, it is the reputed home of violent trolls, so be alert.

Stay: There's really only one obvious choice, and that's the originally-named Dimmuborgir Guesthouse (www.dimmuborgir.is).

Getting there: Guided bus tours are available from Akureyri, or if you choose to drive, it's around a one-hour journey. As always, guided tours are recommended to make the very most of your visit, and to make sure you're safe at all times. If the weather turns, rural lava flows aren't really the kinds of places you want to be caught on your own. Remember those words of Mance Rayder you just read?

GRJÓTAGJÁ

You're bound to recognise this small lava cave near Lake Mývatn. Although the outside may be all snow and ice, the water in the spring here can get up to 50 degrees Celsius, little wonder that Jon Snow and Ygritte chose it to thaw out (let's call it that) after their trek across the wastelands. It has a colourful history for a Jon in real life, too: in the early 18th century, an outlaw named Jón Markússon lived there.

> "I DON'T EVER WANT T' LEAVE THIS CAVE,
> JON SNOW. NOT EVER"
>
> YGRITTE

Getting there: The cave isn't on any guided tours, so you'll have to find it yourself. A headlamp and towel are essentials. Drive east from the village Reykjahlid (Rte 1) for a couple of kilometres and then turn right just before the road to Myvatn Nature Baths. There is a sign to "Grjótagjá" pointing to the gravel road that takes you to the cave. Use the same directions as those to Dimmuborgir from Akureyri – it's an easy stop off on the way.

LAKE MÝVATN

Another easy stop if you're going to do a day tour of the countryside east of Akureyri is this 2300-year-old lake, created by some of the same lava flows. The area has an outstanding array of waterfowl and the entire area is very photographic. They weren't taking in much of the scenery, but this spot was another place where Mance Rayder's wildling horde camped.

Tip: In the summer, the area is overrun by midges, so it's probably best avoided during the warmest months. In fact, the name translates as 'Midge Lake'. So you can't say weren't warned.

3. VATNAJÖKULL NATIONAL PARK

WWW.VATNAJOKULSTHJODGARDUR.IS

This vast National Park is a huge part of Iceland – more than ten percent of its surface area. The world's largest non-polar ice cap, it attracts adventurers, hikers and climbers as well as more casual weekend visitors from Reykjavik, which is around 250km to the west. Visitors can explore the amazing glaciers, caves and waterfalls, as well as taking walks through the forested areas with interpretive guides. The more hardy can even climb Iceland's highest peaks.

The Park has been used for various scenes that take place in the frozen tundra North of the Wall. It is here that the Night's Watch made their dramatic stand against the White Walkers at the Fist of the First Men, the scenes for this battle shot on the Svínafellsjökull glacier. Parts of this part of the park also stood in for other locations in the Frostfangs, the mountain range that covers much of the far north.

> "SAM...WOULD YOU WAKE ME, PLEASE? I AM HAVING THIS TERRIBLE NIGHTMARE."
>
> DOLOROUS EDD, TO SAMWELL TARLY, IN THE MIDST OF THE BATTLE OF THE FIST OF THE FIRST MEN.

Getting there: The Park is a fairly remote, exposed area, so sign up for a guided tour with your hotel or at a local tourist office. Skaftafell is around a 4-hour drive from central Reykjavik. For orientation and information if you're driving under your own steam, head to one of the visitor centres, located in Kirkjubæjarklaustur, Skaftafell and Höfn, Skriðuklaustur or Jökulsárgljúfur.

Stay: There isn't really much to offer in the way of accommodation in the park itself. You can, however, stay at the Visitor Centre Campsite, or Bölti, both in Skaftafell (the park's popular southern section).

Tourism office: www.vatnajokulsthjodgardur.is

TAKE A GOT TOUR: ICELAND

Grayline run tours taking in the dramatic landscape at Þingvellir National Park, the stomping ground of the White Walkers, the trail of the Wildlings from North of the Wall and the settlement-era Viking Lodge at Þjórsárdalur valley. They also boast expert narration throughout the tour. Find out more, including prices, here: http://grayline.is/tours/reykjavik/game-of-thrones-tour-8706_88

Iceland Tours offer full 5-day/4-night tours around the country, with a chance to spend a little more time in each of the locations. The tours are year round, and more details can be found here: https://www.icelandtravel.is/short-breaks/detail/item692630/Game_of_Thrones_-_Iceland:_Beyond_the_Wall/

MALTA

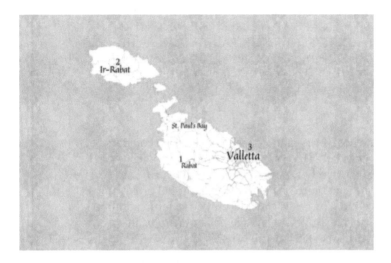

Like a Mediterranean version of Iceland, Malta has a character and history you won't find anywhere else. Together with its sister island Gozo, Malta is home to some of the most impressive historical sights you can imagine – they even rival the fictional descriptions of GoT locations.

Huge monuments rest atop dramatic cliff faces, and underground, a 5000-year old temple is carved right into the rock with amazing artistry.

Mdina is a near-perfectly preserved Medieval city, and so suggested itself with some confidence to the GoT crew as an alternative to Croatia for filming scenes around King's Landing. The capital, Valetta, also served a similar purpose.

The surrounding countryside and coast also played host to the Dothraki, and saw such memorable scenes as Daenerys and Drogo's wedding. The country was used widely for the first season, though filming has not returned to the island since.

Nevertheless, it's a magical destination, especially for keen-eyed fans who are also fans of warm, welcoming climates.

"GROWING UP AT WINTERFELL, ALL I EVER WANTED WAS TO ESCAPE, TO COME HERE, TO THE CAPITAL. TO SEE THE SOUTHERN KNIGHTS AND THEIR PAINTED ARMOUR, AND KING'S LANDING AFTER DARK. ALL THE CANDLES BURNING IN ALL THOSE WINDOWS." SANSA STARK

Tip: The best/best value times to go are the shoulders (just before/after high season) of April–June and September–October. At this time, it's still warm and sunny, though there is the occasional rainfall or hot and humid wind. The sea is considerably warmer in autumn than in spring. Holy Week is a special time to be in Malta, with lots of colourful festivals.

Getting there: Malta International Airport has many European routes, and it's a favourite holiday destination for many nationalities, especially th northern Europeans. If you arrive and aren't renting a car, six express services and other buses serve almost all of Malta's main towns. They depart from the airport, and run from around 5am to midnight.

Tourism office: www.visitmalta.com

1. MDINA & RABAT

These beautiful, medieval walled towns in the centre of the island can trace their history back some 4,000 years. Walking around gives you the feeling of being in a fairytale or mythical adventure, with mazes of narrow, hidden alleyways and lanes trailing off the main streets.

The city was home then, as it still is now to some extent, to Malta's most noble families. With such a rich history, you can imagine they are from diverse lineages - some are descendants of the Norman, some from Sicilian and some from the Spanish.

They were all respective overlords who naturally made Mdina their home from the 12th century onwards, and as their legacy, regally impressive palaces line the city's narrow, shady streets.

According to legend, it was here in 60 A.D. that the Apostle St. Paul was shipwrecked on the Islands and subsequently lived. It is believed that he resided inside the grotto know as Fuori le Mura just outside the city walls of Rabat - now known as St. Paul's Grotto.

You can really imagine the bustle of King's Landing, with mercenaries and spies ducking out of sight. When the Pheonicians settled this area, it was the capital city and known far and wide as The Noble City.

The Romans and the Arabs both added to the fortifications in grand style. They also brought their own touches to the city's culture, though when Valetta became the new capital (as it remains to this present day), Mdina and Rabat became a much more exclusive resort.

Mdina eventually became known as The Silent City - hardly surprising given that less than 300 people are official residents. Nevertheless, this is still a name worthy of a GoT destination, and if you're lucky enough to visit, the hours of tranquillity will only add to the incredibly evocative atmosphere.

Getting there: You can easily travel here from Valetta by bus – service numbers 50, 51, 52 and 53 leave every ten minutes from the capital's bus station, and the journey only takes around 30 minutes or so.

Stay: The Xara Palace Relais & Chateau (www.xarapalace.com.mt) is built around a 17th-century palazzo if you want to stay in luxury. For substantially less, you can stay in equally converted guesthouses such as the Point de Vue or the Casa Melita. Probably the most GoT option, though, is to stay in the Luxury Guard Tower, a place you could easily imagine Littlefinger having an apartment (Google by property name for current guesthouse prices and availability).

See: **Rabat**: St Pauls' Grotto, St Paul's Catacombs, St Agatha's Catacombs, Domus Romana (the Roman House). **Mdina**: The Mdina Dungeons, St Paul's Cathedral and Museum, The Mdina Experience, The Knights of Malta, Bastion Square, Vilhena Palace, Natural History Museum.

Tourism office: www.visitmalta.com/en/mdina-and-rabat

Mdina Gate

The city's glorious main entrance dates back to the early 18th century. The edifice has a Baroque flourish and a coat of arms centring around lions, which also feature on the bridge leading from the gate. The gate makes its screen debut as Catelyn and Rodrik Cassel make their arrival at King's Landing.

Verdala Palace

BUSKETT GARDENS, SIĠĠIEWI

This 16th century former hunting lodge plays host to the great and the good and is a luxurious private residence, though it was used as a military prison by Napoleon. Understandably, the building is not accessible to the public, but you may wander the gardens, and imagine spying on Illyrio Mopatis, seeing as it was his mansion in Season One. This is where Daenerys and Viserys received Khal Drogo.

> "THE WORLD IS ONE GREAT WEB, AND A MAN DARE NOT TOUCH A SINGLE STRAND LEST ALL THE OTHERS TREMBLE."
>
> ILLYRIO MOPATIS

Getting there: The palace is around a 15-minute drive south from the centre of Rabat.

2. GOZO

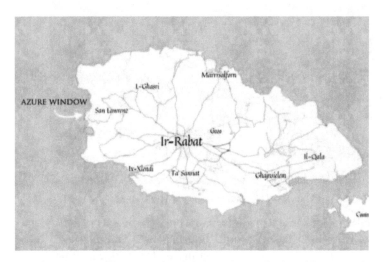

Head to this small, quiet island (*Ghawdex* in the local language) for some well-earned tranquillity. Your likely company will be the scuba divers and snorkelers who come here for the idyllic surrounding waters. There are some truly world class beaches to be found, overlooked by temples and citadels. It's so romantic, in fact, that the location even melted the heart of the Dothraki's fearless leader.

Getting there: A regular ferry service carries passengers and cars between Malta and Gozo (the ports are at, respectively, Cirkewwa and Mgarr. The trip takes about 20 minutes (www.gozochannel.com) and costs around five euros.

Stay: The island has its share of modern hotels, but you can find places with more character, such as the Quaint Boutique Hotel (www.quainthotelsgozo.com), or if you want to spend a little more, there's the world class Kempinski Hotel San Lawrenz (www.kempinksi.com).

See: Mgarr habour, Gran Castello citadel, The Brocktorff Circle, Dwerja, Museum of Archaeology, Victoria (the capital).

Tourism office: www.visitgozo.com

Azure Window

THE AZURE WINDOW (PHOTO VIA CREATIVE COMMONS LICENSE, COURTESY MYRIAM THYES)

This natural limestone rock arch near Dwejra Bay is 100ft high, and unsurprisingly, it attracts scuba divers, snorkelers and even the odd (illegal) cliff diver. DO NOT try this at home. Or in Malta. The 'window' was formed when two caves collapsed, and we're left with a stunning rock formation. Daenerys Targaryen and Khal Drogo's wedding took place here, a rare romantic moment for the hardened warriors (maybe not 'romantic' since she was essentially being sold off, but it's all relative with these barbarians). The spot has a solid cinematic history: as well as Game of Thrones, it also appeared in films such as Clash of the Titans and The Count of Monte Cristo.

> "YER JALAN ATTHIRARI ANNI ("MOON OF MY LIFE" IN DOTHRAKI)"
>
> DROGO
>
> "SHEKH MA SHIERAKI ANNI ("MY SUN AND STARS" IN DOTHRAKI)"
>
> DAENERYS

Tip: Visitors can explore the site by foot or rent a small boat at the nearby Inland Sea to view this wonder from the ocean.

3. VALLETTA

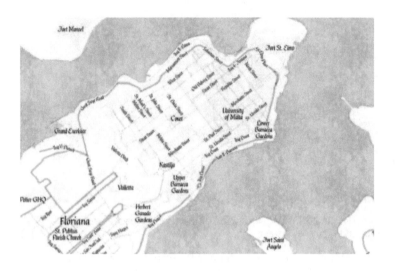

Possibly the world's smallest capital city, Valletta is just 600m by 1000m in size, and was built 'by gentlemen for gentlemen' by the Knights of St John in the 16th and 17th centuries. However, enough historic wonders are packed into the small space for UNESCO to deem it a World Heritage Site, and it is impressive enough for the GoT crew to cast it to represent parts of King's Landing.

Stay: The compact size of the 'city' means few accommodation options, but the Grand Harbour Hotel (www.grandharbourhotel.com) and the Castille Hotel (www.hotelcastillemalta.com) are among the best in town.

See: Marsamxsett Harbour, Grand Harbour, Republic Street, Barracca Gardens, Grandmaster's Palace and Armoury, St Paul's Shipwreck Church, National Museum of Fine Arts, National War Museum, Mesquita Square.

Tourism office: www.visitmalta.com/en/valletta

Fort Manoel

This great fortification stands on Manoel Island in Marsamxett Harbour, just north-west of Valletta. It was built as an active military base by the Knights of Malta in the early-to-mid 18th century and it played an dramatic and important role during World War Two. It also has a notorious role in GoT as the Great Sept of Baelor, the infamous spot where Joffrey has Ned Stark admit to being a traitor. He then gives him a lovely gift. Wait, sorry, actually he has him executed in front of everyone.

> "My mother wishes me to let Lord Eddard join the Night's Watch. Stripped of all titles and powers, he would serve the realm in permanent exile. And my Lady Sansa has begged mercy for her father. But they have the soft hearts of women. So long as I am your king, treason shall never go unpunished. Sir Ilyn, bring me his head!"
>
> Joffrey Baratheon

Fort Ricasoli

You can't actually visit this crumbling 17th century fortification built by the Knights of Malta. However, you can't really miss it if you pay a visit to the scenic village of Kalkara and look up to the spookily-named Gallows Point. The fort dominates the views of the Grand Harbour. Sadly, it was badly damaged during World War Two, but this didn't stop it making an appearance in historical films such as Troy, Gladiator, Helen of Troy and Julius Caesar. Back in the TV world of Westeros, Fort Ricasoli was used to represent the Red Keep in King's Landing.

Getting there: Take a taxi around the peninsula to Kalkara – it's only a 15-20 minute ride.

Fort St Angelo

The walled town of Birgu is only a few minutes' drive from Valletta, and this ancient fort is the main attraction. It was yet another military installation for the British during World War II, and was the seat of the Knights of Malta, so it has a prestigious heritage. According to some historians, the site was originally a Roman settlement, so its story stretches back even further.

The underground tunnels where Arya chases a cat in the Red Keep currently cannot be visited, but there are some good photo opportunities for capturing the exterior from around the town.

> "The Red Keep has ways known only to ghosts and spiders."
> Varys

Getting there: Again, the simplest thing is to take a taxi from Valetta. It's very close to Kalkara, so it's easy to combine a visit to both these places at once.

SAN ANTON PALACE

Located in Attard (25 minutes west of Valletta by car), this 16th century palace is none other than the official residence of the President of Malta. It was originally built by The Knight Antoine de Paule in the 18th century as a luxurious villa for himself and his guests. It has since received such luminaries as Queen Elizabeth II on royal visits, so as you can imagine, there's little hope of commoners such as us getting a look inside. However, the beautiful gardens are open to the public and you can catch glimpses of the grounds, which played the part of the Red Keep in Season One. It was here that the Starks first arrive and with typical Lannister hospitality, their attendants are murdered by soldiers while unloading cargo. The Palace also houses the Red Keep's Hallway, where scenes of intrigue between Ned, Varys and Littlefinger take place.

> "IS EVERYONE SOMEONE'S INFORMER IN
> THIS CURSED CITY?"
>
> EDDARD STARK, ABOUT KING'S LANDING

TAKE A GOT TOUR: MALTA

Viator runs a full-day tour, picking up from your hotel. It covers Mdina, the perfectly preserved medieval city, and the backdrop for the Seven Kingdom's capital of King's Landing (including the Red Keep). There are photo stops at the Great Sept of Baelor, the Game of Thrones church in Gzira (scenes include the wedding of King Joffrey to Margaery Tyrell), Fort St Elmo (used as Sowbelly Row during season one), the King's Landing Skull Chamber in Birgu and the spot where Ned Stark confronted his rival Cersei Lanister in the Godswood. You'll continue to Kalkara to see the 17th-century fortress that provided the setting for Red Keep's gates. After lunch, you can visit the courtyard of Illyrios Palace where the Stark family discovered a stag killed by a dire wolf. From there, it's on to the walled city of Mdina and walk around its main gate, pretty streets and the atmospheric Mesquita Square. See several different locations that featured in King's Landing including the famous Tower of the Hand. More info: http://bit.ly/1gVjO2h

MOROCCO

For Season Three, the GoT cast and crew took their first programme-related steps outside of Europe, to the sun-kissed North African country of Morocco. There is much to recommend the choice, Morocco being one of Africa's most diverse nations, and its ancient cities, with their distinctive medinas (old Arabian quarters) and souqs (traditional open-air markets). The location team chose three distinct places, one of them admittedly a huge film studio, to represent scenes that took place in and around Astapor, Yunkai and Pentos.

> "ANCIENT AND GLORIOUS IS YUNKAI.
> OUR EMPIRE WAS OLD BEFORE DRAGONS
> STIRRED IN OLD VALYRIA."
>
> RAZDAL MO ERA

1. AÏT-BEN-HADDOU

This fortified city (known locally as a *ksar* – do we hear a touch of Dothraki? No?) lies along the ancient caravan road that leads out from the Sahara Desert to the capital city of Marrakech.

The oldest parts of the town are made from clay, and are one of the world's most impressive examples of this kind of architecture. The town is really a collection of six huge Kasbahs (citadels) and fifty individual *ksars*, and it was pronounced a UNESCO World Heritage Site in 1987.

In the GoT universe, Aït-Ben-Haddou depicts Yunkai, which is the smallest of the three cities in Slaver's Bay, and Pentos, which is the biggest of the Free Cities. You should recognise it as the backdrop to Daenerys Targaryen's adventures through Slaver's Bay.

It should be even more familiar to film buffs, since it has a proud history of being a location for big-budget productions, including Lawrence of Arabia, Jesus of Nazareth, The Mummy, Gladiator, Time Bandits, Babel and The Living Daylights.

"PENTOS IS THE MOST RUTHLESS. THE
MAGISTERS MAKE A GREAT SHOW OF
CHOOSING THE PRINCE OF PENTOS FROM
THE GREAT FAMILIES, AND GRANTING HIM
THE POWERS OF TRADE, JUSTICE AND
WAR...AS LONG AS HE CHECKS WITH THEM
FIRST."

SER JORAH MORMONT

Tip: The town itself is the main attraction, with mud buildings
climbing up the side of the hill – you have to walk and climb a
little to see them. The Granary at the top of the hill is well
worth the effort, though be careful of any 'entrepreneurs'
trying to assist you unnecessarily.

Getting there: Aït Benhaddou is easily accessible from
Marrakesh. The journey is around three hours and though
busses are available (on the Marrakech-Ouarzazate route), it's
best to book a tour via your hotel or a local tourism office. You
can combine it with a tour of the Atlas studios at Ouazarzate as
they are only a 30-minute drive away from each other.

Stay: You can't go too far wrong with the views from the
accommodations here. The Auberge Bagdad Café (www.hotel-
ait-ben-haddou.com) gets rave reviews for its charming service
and the Kasbah Tebi (www.kasbah-tebi.com) is about as
magical a place as you can lay your head.

See: Tamdaght Kasbah, Hotel la Kasbah, Oued Ounilla
Riverbed, Mausoleum of Ben-Haddou, The Granary (at the top
of the hill).

2. ESSAOUIRA

There's a slightly European – even French look to the fishing harbour of Essaouira, but once inside the city walls, you're firmly in Morrocco.

It's a relatively laid-back kind of place, awash with surfers and windsurfers (the gusts of wind here are great for tricks out on the waves, not so much for a picnic on the beach) and artists.

It's also a resort that hasn't yet been completely overrun by rampant tourism, so it still feels like you're making something of a discovery.

You can trace the relaxed vibes right back to the 1960s, when it was something of a hippie hangout for cool cats such as Jimi Hendrix.

Its fishing port credentials means there's a limitless supply (or at least, more than you can eat) of tasty, fresh seafood, so be sure to hunt down some of the restaurants near the waterfront.

The old sandstone ramparts are perfect for the city of Astapor, famously the place where Daenerys Targaryen truly started to make waves. It's here that she freed an army of slaves, in the process delivering justice to their evil owner, in the shape of a fiery dragon blast to the face.

> "ASTAPOR IS MOST BEAUTIFUL AT DUSK, YOUR GRACE. THE GOOD MASTERS LIGHT SILK LANTERNS ON EVERY TERRACE, SO ALL THE PYRAMIDS GLOW WITH COLORED LIGHTS. PLEASURE BARGES PLY THE WORM, PLAYING SOFT MUSIC AND CALLING AT THE LITTLE ISLANDS FOR FOOD AND WINE AND OTHER DELIGHTS."
>
> MISSANDEI, TO DAENERYS TARGARYEN

Tip: Come here in winter, when the town is at its most dramatic, and not too busy with domestic Moroccan tourists.

Getting there: It's around a two and a half hour drive from Marrakech, so you can either hire a private driver, or hire your own car. There are several options for taking buses, too – ask a local travel agent or your hotel for the current schedules and prices.

Stay: The accommodation choices are a mix between trendy new boutique hotels, traditional riads and trendy boutique hotels trying to look like traditional riads. Riad Baladin (www.riadbaladin.com) has had near-impeccable reviews since it opened, and Dar Al Bahar (www.daralbahar.com) gives you the touch of authenticity you might be looking for. Prices skyrocket during the summer.

See: The souk, the fish market, the Portuguese Ramparts.

Tourism office: www.essaouira.nu/tourism

3. Ouarzazate

Welcome to the Hollywood of Morocco. Well, maybe not in terms of lifestyle, but definitely in terms of heritage, as this ancient Berber town is home to Atlas Studios – the world's (physically) largest film studios. This former trading post is in the High Atlas Mountains on the edge of the desert, and has been the location for a list of movies as long as your arm. A few of the more famous ones include: The Living Daylights, Asterix & Obelix, Lawrence of Arabia, The Man Who Would Be King, Kingdom of Heaven and Babel. Together with Aït Benhaddou, the studio and surrounds stood in for Pentos, again a well-used location for many of the scenes of Daenerys Targaryen and her ascent to power.

> "I will not come to Pentos bowl in hand."
>
> Daenerys Targaryen to Arstan Whitebeard

Getting there: Unless you really want to undertake the two and a half hour drive out into the mountains under your own steam, it's much easier to book a tour in Marrakech, either through your hotel or through a local tour operator. It's a much easier trip from Aït Benhaddou, just 30 minutes away.

Stay: You'll probably want to stay in Aït Ben Haddou (see above) and take a day tour from there.

Tip: See the studio website for more detail on the tours. Actual GoT sets will obviously not be available to see, but it is impressive in its own right. www.studiosatlas.com

Take a GoT tour: Morocco

At the time of writing, there were no organised tours of GoT sites in Morocco. It can only be a matter of time before this changes, so watch this space. Or the internet.

NORTHERN IRELAND

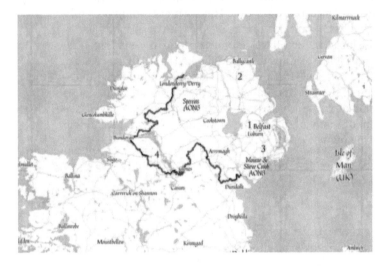

No other country has been so positively affected by the production of GoT than Northern Ireland. Within living memory, Belfast at least wasn't a destination you would really consider visiting. It was a city torn apart by sectarian violence and had intimidating amounts of armed forces patrolling the streets.

Modern day Belfast, by contrast, is a truly wonderful city. It brims over with vitality and charm, and has history, nightlife and scenery to woo even the most sceptical of visitors. Hip bars and hotels, a newly-developed waterfront and locals that are enjoying every minute of the city's new life are what you'll find.

The opening of Titanic Belfast in 2012 was a major draw for tourism, and who would have thought that over a century ago, the construction of the world's most infamous ship would indirectly lead to a flourishing film industry and spaces that would house a TV phenomenon? Yes, the interior locations for GoT are mostly shot at Titanic Studios, inside the vast Paint

Hall, a huge warehouse once used for work on the ships built by Harland and Wolff, the company that launched the Titanic in 1912.

Naomi Liston, who works in the show's locations department, took part in a panel discussion in Belfast "It's one of the most beautiful places," she said, talking about the show's decision to make is home there. "Is it cost effective? Does the area offer evocative filming locations? Does it have studio space? Northern Ireland ticked all the boxes."

1. BELFAST

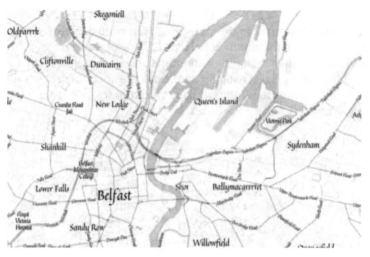

Belfast took an inspired decision to spend time and money paying homage to its shipbuilding history. The focal point, Titanic Belfast, is touted billed as the world's largest Titanic visitor experience, with nine galleries illustrating the Titanic's story, from its construction to its dramatic end.

The Titanic Studios encompass the Paint Hall studio and two state of the art, 24,000-square-foot sound stages that have been used from the beginning of Season Three. Sadly, GoT fans can't freely tour the studios, but you can easily see the exteriors from Titanic Belfast.

Getting there: Belfast International Airport is well connected to European flight routes.

Stay: The Merchant Hotel (www.themerchanthotel.com) and The Europa (www.hastingshotels.com/europa-belfast) are rightfully the best known, but budget options such as the Premier Inn (www.premierinn.com) are just as well located.

See: Titanic Belfast, Ulster Museum, St Anne's Cathedral, Cathedral Quarter, Queen's University, Botanic Gardens.

Tourism office: www.visit-belfast.com

2. COUNTY ANTRIM

Breathtaking is an easy word to bandy around, but it's completely appropriate in this neck of the woods. Scenic spots really don't get more impressive than Giant's Causeway and the Carrick-a-Rede Rope Bridge.

Northern Ireland's star natural attractions really are world class, and the walk along the Causeway Coast Way between the two sights is a bucket-list experience. These gorgeous cliffs and swathes of sandy coastline have been a for GoT locations.

The picturesque village of Ballintoy doubled as Lordsport on Pyke, the island base for the Greyjoy clan and the rest of the Iron Islands residents. The cute harbour town of Ballycastle was birthplace of the eunuch with the vast network of spies, Varys (the Free City).

If you stray inland, with some detective work, you can find the Dark Hedges Road (or the Kingsroad, as you'll more likely know it by) and as you near Ballymoney, you can experience the dramatic scenery that enveloped Arya Stark as she craftily eluded evil King Joffrey's soldiers.

See: Giant's Causeway, Glens of Antrim, Portrush

Tourism Office: www.discovernorthernireland.com

BALLINTOY HARBOUR

This picturesque little fishing village is locally known as 'The Raised Beach' and its coastline and harbour stand out, even along the relentlessly lovely coast of Antrim.

The harbour can be found at the end of a steep but narrow road that runs down from down Knocksaughey Hill. This road passes by the entrance to Larrybane and the famous Carrick-a-Rede Rope Bridge. Ballintoy village itself is just a ten-minute walk from the harbour, and is peppered with cute shops and a couple of old churches, with Ballintoy Parish Church overlooking the harbour from atop the hill.

Ballintoy Harbour should be recognisable as the port of Pyke, famed for being the cove where Theon Greyjoy first arrives back in the Iron Islands and where he later has to wrangle his crew and admires his charmingly named ship, the Sea Bitch. This is also where he first meets his sister Yara.

> "I'M A GREYJOY. WE'VE BEEN LORDS OF THE IRON ISLANDS FOR HUNDREDS OF YEARS. THERE'S NOT A FAMILY IN WESTEROS THAT CAN LOOK DOWN ON US. NOT EVEN THE LANNISTERS." THEON GREYJOY

Getting there: Ballintoy is just over an hour's drive north of Belfast via the M2, A26 and A44 roads.

Stay: If you're on a budget and just need a bed for the night, you could do worse than the 4-star Whitepark Bay Youth Hostel www.hini.org.uk). There are dozens of Bed and Breakfast-style cottages, stand outs including the 150-year old converted fisherman's cottage, Braeside Cottage. The Fullerton Arms is also a cosy guesthouse and restaurant with great views (Google by name for latest rates and availability)

See: Fishermen erected the Carrick-a-Rede Rope Bridge to Carrick-a-Rede island some 350 years ago. It stretches over a 23m (69ft) -deep and 20m (60ft)-wide chasm. You may not want to look down.

CUSHENDUN CAVES

400 million years in the making, the stunning Cushendun Caves are the eroded remains of a mountain range. Cushendun itself is a tiny village of only around 150 people, and the area has belonged to the National Trust since 1954 and as such is a well-preserved region of natural beauty. It has historically been a well-used landing spot and ferry route to Scotland - the Mull of Kintyre can be seen across the water on clear days.

The caves themselves are easily reached, though you can get detailed information from the visitors' centre at Larnes. The road from here takes visitors past some spectacular costal scenery as it wends its way along to Loughan Bay, Torr Head and Ballycastle. Just outside the village are the ruins of 14th century Castle Carra.

The caves and little stretch of coast surrounding them were the backdrop to one of the more memorable scenes in the show. It was here that Davos Seaworth (following orders from Stannis Baratheon) landed ashore with the red priestess Melisandre, and where she gave birth to the shadow demon that kills Renly. In GoT world this area is referred to as the Stormlands.

Getting there: The caves are around an hour's drive north of Belfast, via the M2 and A26 roads.

The Dark Hedges

If there was any one place you had to pick to say it was right out of a fantasy tale, then it would probably be this magical avenue of ancient beech trees.

They lay in wait between the sleepy towns of Ballycastle and Ballymoney and are rightly one of the most photographed sites in the country.

This would undoubtedly please the Stuart family, who planted them in the 18th century to impress visitors to their Georgian mansion, Gracehill House. They did the job so well that it's still impressing people to this day and will hopefully do so for centuries to come.

The road you're looking for is Bregagh Road, just off the B147 (through the unlikely-named village of Stranocum). Keep your foot off the gas pedal as you approach, just so you can get the absolute most of what Shakespeare may have called 'a most excellent canopy' (yes I know he was talking about the sky, but let's go with it).

The trees flank you, with their stand longest branches reaching out over your head and intertwining in the most enchantingly satisfactory fashion.

In Westeros, this evocative avenue is, of course, the Kingsroad, which leads north out of King's Landing. Disguising herself as a boy, Arya escapes along this road from the city with Yoren, Gendry and Hot Pie. Arya was, of course, in a cart. Bonus points for doing it the same way.

BRIENNE OF TARTH: "NO ONE'S SEEN ARYA STARK SINCE HER FATHER WAS BEHEADED. SHE'S PRESUMED DEAD."

HOT PIE: "SHE WEREN'T WHEN I LAST SPOKE TO HER. HEADING UP NORTH WITH THE NIGHT'S WATCH. SHE WAS ALL DRESSED UP AS A BOY...GOING BY THE NAME 'ARRY. "

BRIENNE OF TARTH: "SO WHAT HAPPENED TO HER? THE QUICK VERSION. "

HOT PIE: "THE LANNISTERS TOOK US PRISONER. WE ESCAPED. THE BROTHERHOOD TOOK US PRISONER. THEY 'SOLD' ME TO THE INNKEEP. THEY WERE GONNA SELL ARYA TO HER MOTHER AT RIVERRUN, ALONG WITH ANOTHER PRISONER: BIG UGLY FELLOW, FOUL MOUTH AND A FACE LIKE A HALF-BURNT HAM. NOT FRIENDLY."

Getting there: The Dark Hedges are around 2.5 miles from the village of Stranocum, heading north.Stranocum is about an hour's drive north of Belfast, via the M2, A26 and A44 roads.

DUNSEVERIK

A small hamlet near the Giant's Causeway, it was nevertheless home to a substantial castle, sadly destroyed by the Scottish army in the 17th century. Surrounded by ocean on three sides, it remains a wonderfully scenic vantage point, and some of the ancient ruins still remain.

The location was used during the tense stand-off between Renly and Stannis Baratheon as they both talked up their claims to the Iron Throne.

> STANNIS BARATHEON: THE IRON THRONE IS MINE. BY RIGHT. ALL THOSE THAT DENY THAT ARE MY FOES.

> RENLY BARATHEON: THE WHOLE REALM DENIES IT FROM DORNE TO THE WALL. OLD MEN DENY IT WITH THEIR DEATH RATTLE AND UNBORN CHILDREN DENY IT IN THEIR MOTHERS' WOMBS. NO ONE WANTS YOU FOR THEIR KING. YOU NEVER WANTED ANY FRIENDS, BROTHER, BUT A MAN WITHOUT FRIENDS IS A MAN WITHOUT POWER.

> STANNIS BARATHEON: FOR THE SAKE OF THE MOTHER WHO BORE US, I WILL GIVE YOU THIS ONE NIGHT TO RECONSIDER. STRIKE YOUR BANNERS, COME TO ME BEFORE DAWN, AND I WILL GRANT YOU YOUR OLD SEAT IN THE COUNCIL. I'LL EVEN NAME YOU MY HEIR... UNTIL A SON IS BORN TO ME. OTHERWISE, I SHALL DESTROY YOU.

Getting there: It's around a 90-minute drive north from Belfast, but through some of the most wonderful County Antrim scenery, so it doesn't feel too much of a stretch.

LARRYBANE

Along the beautiful Northern Irish coast, this glorious patch of coast is protected by Sheep Island and a shallow reef, making Larrybane one of the most sheltered locations in the north. The entire stretch is absolutely stunning.

Sheep Island is a designated Special Protection Area and Area of Special Scientific Interest as it is home to a number of a particular species of cormorant.

The Larrybane area is part of The Stormlands in GoT. You may recognise it as the spot where King Renly sets up camp and where the tournament takers place in which Brienne of Tarth is victorious against Ser Loras Tyrell.

> "WHERE IS IT WRITTEN THAT POWER IS THE SOLE PROVINCE OF THE WORST? THAT THRONES ARE ONLY MADE FOR THE HATED AND THE FEARED? YOU WOULD BE A WONDERFUL KING." LORAS TYRELL TO RENLY BARATHEON

Stay: Ballintoy is the best place to stay for seeing Larrybane.

MAGHERAMORNE QUARRY

This disused quarry actually hosted two film sets. The first was a reconstruction of Castle Black and the house in which Jon Snow lives as part of the Guard at night. The nearby lake also served as the set for HardHome, the backdrop for the spectacular battle in Season Five. While you can visit the small village, there isn't much to see when the sets aren't built up there, and it is of course very dangerous to explore quarries without supervision, so stick to what you can see from the road. It's not too much, sadly.

> "HE'S PRETTIER THAN BOTH MY DAUGHTERS, BUT HE KNOWS HOW TO FIGHT. HE'S YOUNG, BUT HE KNOWS HOW TO LEAD. HE CAME BECAUSE HE NEEDS US, AND WE NEED HIM."
> TORMUND, TO THE ELDERS AT HARDHOME, ABOUT JON SNOW

Tip: Magheramorne is around five miles south of Larne. It's just over 30 minutes' drive north from Belfast, via the A2 road.

MUSSENDEN TEMPLE AND DOWNHILL BEACH

Some eight miles of golden sands make up Downhill beach and surround this beautiful area. The town is best known for the Mussenden Temple, a distinctive-looking round temple that was originally built to be a summer library. It stands defiantly and dramatically on the top of a cliff, looking out across the panoramic Northern Irish coast.

Both the Mussenden Temple and Downhill Beach were used in GoTh as the location for the Dragonstone exterior. The ritual burning of the old gods by Melisandre took place here, as did the scene where Stannis Baratheon draws the flaming sword 'Lightbringer' from the flames.

> "THE NIGHT IS DARK AND FULL OF TERRORS...BUT THE FIRE BURNS THEM ALL AWAY." MELISANDRE

Tip: This is an easy day trip from Ballintoy, just a 40-minute drive each way.

3. COUNTY DOWN

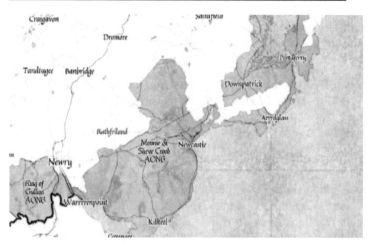

Lush fields, gleaming loughs and heather-flecked peaks surround you as you wander about this affluent region. It's a popular weekend away for city folk, with golf courses and gourmet restaurants aplenty.

The views are for everyone, though, and with the ancient castles and monasteries, County Down can be a somewhat haunting region. The Mourne Mountains loom above you, granite hills with whitewashed cottages and flower patches.

Adventurous hikers (and would-be Night's Watch apprentices) can cross the hills and on through Tollymore Forest Park before ending up in the old seaside town of Newcastle.

For GoT fans, this is where it all began. The very opening sequence sees a patrol north of the Wall meet a messy end in Tollymor Forest. Castle Ward and Inch Abbey will be all too familiar for fans of House Stark and there are also very memorable and scenic backdrops to the Iron Islands.

Getting there: The entire county is easily driveable from a base in Belfast.

See: Mourne Mountains, Newcastle, Slieve Croob, Newry

Tourism Office: www.visitnorthernirleand.com

CASTLE WARD

This grand house was built in the 1760s at the behest of Lord and Lady Bangor. They reportedly both had very strong personalities that didn't always sit in agreement with each other, and their different tastes in architecture resulted in a strange mix of styles.

Visitors can see a Victorian laundry museum, the Strangford Lough Wildlife Centre, Old Castle Ward (a 16th-century Plantation tower) and Castle Audley (a 15th-century tower house), as well as exploring the walking and cycling trails.

The older parts of the Estate stood in for Winterfell in several episodes. It took over the role from Doune Castle in Scotland, which was only used for the pilot episode (which has never aired). Castle Ward was used for various scenes of sparring in Winterfell's castle yard and the arrival of King Robert's formal visit with his entourage. The rest of the castle's interior shots were filmed at the Paint Hall studio facility in Belfast.

> "HE REMEMBERED WINTERFELL AS HE HAD LAST SEEN IT. NOT AS GROTESQUELY HUGE AS HARRENHAL, NOR AS SOLID AND IMPREGNABLE TO LOOK AT AS STORM'S END, YET THERE HAD BEEN A GREAT STRENGTH IN THOSE STONES, A SENSE THAT WITHIN THOSE WALLS A MAN MIGHT FEEL SAFE."
>
> TYRION LANNISTER'S THOUGHTS ON THE CASTLE OF HOUSE STARK.

Getting there: The castle is seven miles north-east of Downpatrick, and one mile from Strangford on the A25 road. From Belfast, the drive takes just under an hour, heading south on the A24 and A7 roads.

Inch Abbey & The Quoile River

This ancient site is located on the north bank of the Quoile River, and was founded by John de Courcy as an atonement for his destruction another abbey at Erenagah. It is believed that the buildings are mainly from the 12th and 13th centuries.

In GoT world, Inch Abbey is featured as the Riverlands, where the army of the north wait to cross the River Trident. It is here that Robb and Caitlin Stark learn of Ned Stark's execution. The banks of the Quoile River, which runs through part of the Abbey's estate, have appeared as the location of The Twins, home of Walder Frey, and the scene in which Jaime Lannister and Brienne of Tarth find three women hanging from a tree.

> "Memories of ancient wrongs and bygone betrayals were not oft put aside by the lords of the Trident, whose enmities ran as deep as the rivers that watered their lands."
>
> The writings of Yandel

Getting there: The abbey is located off A7 road, a mile northwest of Downpatrick, or an hour south of Belfast.

Murlough Bay

This extraordinary stretch of dune landscape - hauntingly located at the edge of Dundrum Bay and the Mourne Mountains - has developed its beauty over 6,000 years. A fragile but spectacular sand system, it is owned and maintained by the National Trust, and was opened as Ireland's very first nature reserve in 1967.

Visitors can walk the network of paths and boardwalks through the dunes, which turn into woodland and heath as you explore further. Depending on the season, you'll be treated to a vast array of butterflies and wild flowers, and at the end of it all, you can sit and drink in one of the finest beaches in the country. On clear days, there are views across the waters to the Mull of Kintyre, Islay, Rathlin and various other Scottish islands.

Murlough Bay stars in Season Three, where it was used as a setting for the Iron Islands. It is where Theon and his sister Yara ride horses, and also where Davos Seaworth finds himself washed ashore after the Battle of Blackwater Bay.

Getting there: From Belfast, the bay is about 25 miles south on the A24. Newry is 25 miles west and Downpatrick is 10 miles to the east, both on the A25.

TOLLYMORE FOREST PARK

These 630 hectares at the foot of the Mourne Mountains are a hub for outdoor activities. Hiking, climbing and horse riding all take place in and around the trails that lead through some of the region's most breathtaking scenery.

Within the forest there are several follies (ornamental buildings with no real purpose), such as a barn dressed to resemble a church, gothic style gate arches and stone cones atop gate piers. There is a selection of walking trails along the banks of the River Shimna, all marked by rocky outcrops, bridges, grottos and caves.

The forest features several times in some key scenes in GoT. In the opening scenes, it is here that a member of the Night's Watch sees a family of Wildlings dead on the snow and encounters a White Walker. This is also where the Stark men find the direwolf pups. Later on, a terrified Theon Greyjoy is chased on horseback by Ramsay Snow, the Bastard of Bolton.

WAYMAR ROYCE: WHAT DO YOU EXPECT? THEY'RE SAVAGES. ONE LOT STEALS A GOAT FROM ANOTHER LOT, AND BEFORE YOU NOW IT, THEY'RE RIPPING EACH OTHER TO PIECES.

WILL: I NEVER SEEN WILDLINGS DO A THING LIKE THIS. I NEVER SEEN A THING LIKE THIS, NOT EVER IN MY LIFE!

WAYMAR ROYCE: HOW CLOSE DID YOU GET?

WILL: CLOSE AS ANY MAN WOULD.

Getting there: The forest, and the Tollymore National Outdoor Centre, are around an hour's drive south of Belfast via the A29 and A24 roads.

4. COUNTY FERMANAGH

MARBLE ARCH CAVES

The full name of this natural wonder is the Marble Arch Caves Global Geopark. It's an extensive, spectacular maze of underground passages that attract adventurous tourists and actual underground explorers alike.

As a member of the public, you can visit with only minor amounts of an intrepid nature necessary. The official guided tour lasts around 75 minutes and involves a short boat journey and a guided walk of about 1.5km/1 mile, with 160 steps to climb at the end. Full and half day tours for the very curious are also offered by the centre.

The caves feature when Arya was captured and dragged to the Brotherhood without Banners' hideout. This spooky spot is otherwise known to us as Pollnagollum Cave.

Getting there: The caves are a two-hour drive west from Belfast, using the M1 and A4 roads.

TAKE A GOT TOUR: NORTHERN IRLELAND

Game of Thrones Tours run two full-day location tours, one from Belfast and one from Dublin. Both take in a coach tour and two 'location treks'.

From Belfast: The coach heads past Scrabo Tower, before driving down the Ards Peninsula. The first main stop is at Winterfell, where you can see nine GoT locations. The coach supplies costumes if you want to take some memorable photos. From there, it's lunch and then a photo stop at Inch Abbey (where Robb's bannermen pledge fealty to the King in the North). An afternoon trek around Tollymore Forest before driving back through the Mourne Mountains.

From Dublin: The tour takes in the same locations and treks, though the order is reversed. For the latest prices and schedules, go to www.gameofthronestours.com

SCOTLAND

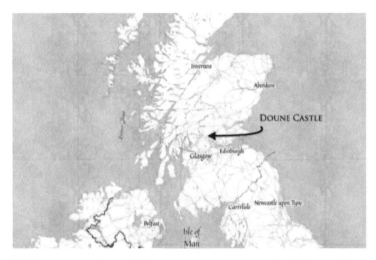

Sadly, only one Scottish location was ever used in GoT, and it didn't make it onto the screen before Northern Ireland was settled on. It seems a shame, especially since Hadrian's Wall is such an obvious influence (though it is not quite of the same awe-inspiring dimensions as The Wall – more on this later).

In any case, fans will still find the trip to Scotland worthwhile, especially if they are visiting places that witnessed some of the real life events that inspired GoT plotlines – some of the gorier battles between the clans were later further dramatised by George RR Martin (The Red Wedding being of particular note – again, more on this later).

Getting there: Flights into either Glasgow or Edinburgh will serve you well for visiting nearby Stirling.

Stay: One of the most historic inns is The Portcullis (www.theprtcullishotel.com) - it is almost in the shadow of Stirling Castle.

See: Stirling Castle

DOUNE CASTLE

One for the GoT completists among you, here. This 13th to 14th-century medieval stronghold just outside Stirling was originally built by the Duke of Albany, Robert Stewart. He was ruler of Scotland from 1388 until his death in 1420.

By great fortune, and testament to how well it was built, the castle has survived in excellent condition and remains almost completely unchanged until the present day.

Doune Castle has enjoyed lots of on-screen time, and can be seen in films such as Monty Python and the Holy Grail, as well as the famous classical adaptation of Ivanhoe that starred Elizabeth Taylor.

The castle was used as the set for Winterfell in the pilot episode for Game of Thrones. According to the website gameofthroneswikia.com, "The Game of Thrones pilot episode was the first episode of the series filmed, but has never been aired. The pilot was shot between 24 October and 19 November 2009, and was directed by Thomas McCarthy.

A re-shot version of the pilot, directed by Tim Van Patten, serves as the first episode of the series itself. It is not known if the original pilot will ever be screened or released."

In truth, you're not seeing anything that has been on screen, but it's still pretty exciting to search out one of the original televisual inspirations for Winterfell.

Tip: You can discover the nature trail in the castle grounds or take an audio tour of the castle, narrated by Monty Python's own Terry Jones.

Getting there: Stirling can be reached easily by train from Edinburgh (90 minutes) and Glasgow (45 minutes). From Stirling bus station, take Addison News bus no 1 to Doune, Main street library. Walk 8 mins to Doune Castle. If you're driving, take the A84 north from Stirling and look for signs at around 15km/10miles.

Stay: There are some beautifully historic accommodation options in Doune, most of them privately rented or Bed and Breakfast properties. The best are Glenardoch House and Brambles Apartment. The Red Lion Inn is also a solid choice.

TAKE A GOT TOUR: SCOTLAND

Black Kilt Tours offers a personal tour of Doune Castle. They can also arrange trips to Glen Coe - The Glencoe Massacre (1692) was the inspiration for the Red Wedding. More info: www.black-kilt-tours.org/scotland-in-film

SPAIN

It wasn't until the introduction of the fictional city of Dorne in Season Five that Spain joined the illustrious ranks of countries serving as GoT locations.

The production team chose Spain to play host to the southernmost cities of the Seven Kingdoms. At this point of Season Five, filming was –almost unbelievably - taking place in four countries simultaneously, an impressive feat for any TV show.

The memorably spectacular cities of Dorne and Volantis were both filmed here, and the historic, southern Spanish cities of Cordoba and Seville were chosen to represent them. At the time of writing, Season Six was already casting for extras in the city of Girona (in the North), so look for more Spanish flare.

Bernadette Caufield, GoT executive producer, told Variety in an interview, "Seville opened its doors to us and we were honoured by that. Nothing was impossible and that is gloriously reflected on screen. We also loved shooting in Osuna where we were welcomed and cared for like a long-lost loved one. The time spent in Osuna will stay with our cast and crew forever."

1. CORDOBA

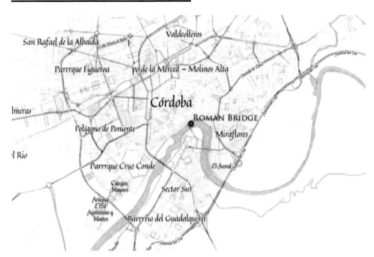

Cordoba is architecturally exciting, with the magnificent Mezquita (a decorous and lavish mosque) lording it over the skyline. The medieval city, just north of the river bend, is a maze of evocative narrow streets – little wonder they caught the eye of the GoT team as they looked to bring Volantis to life. Here you'll find historic Jewish, Muslim and Christian Quarters, each with their own charms and with old bodegas and souvenir shops enough for any visitor.

Getting there: The nearest airports are Seville, Jerez, Malaga and Granada, all less than three hours away – bus services and taxis all run frequently.

Stay: The (5 star) Hospes Palacio del Bailio (www.hospes.com) is in a spectacular location and is a 16th century wonder. Alma Andalusia (www.hospederiaalmaandalusi.com) delivers modern design at more affordable prices.

See: The Mezquita, Alcazar de Reyes Cristianos, Synagogue, Calle de las Flores, Plaza de la Corredra, city walls.

Tourism Office: www.cordobatourismo.com

The Roman bridge

The Roman Bridge in Cordoba was built by imperial troops in the first century BC. It has 16 arches, is 247 metres long and stands across the Guadalquivir River. The towers were added at a later date, sometime in the 16th century. The bridge is a beautiful reflection of the Moorish architecture style of the city and although much of the masonry that you see here was added in a restoration in 2006, there are still – unbelievably – some original arches (the 14th and 15th ones).

> TALISA MAEGYR: "WHAT IF I TOLD YOU MY FATHER SOLD LACE ON THE LONG BRIDGE AND MY MOTHER, MY BROTHER, AND I LIVED WITH HIM ABOVE OUR SHOP?"
>
> ROBB STARK: "I'D CALL YOU A LIAR."

The bridge became the Long Bridge in the Free City of Volantis. Tyrion Lannister and Varys take a walk on the bridge as they arrive from Pentos. Tyrion insists on exploring (he was getting antsy in the carriage) and they walk around the bridge and surrounding neighbourhood before Tyrion ducks in to a brothel. I know, classic Tyrion.

2. Seville & Osuna

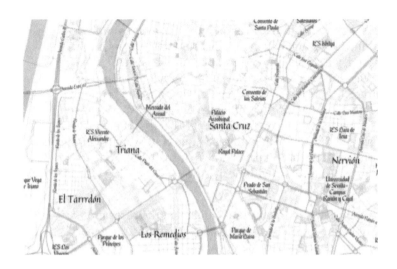

According to myth, Seville was founded around 3,000 years ago by none other than the god Hercules. Whatever the legends, the truth is that the city has retained its strong personality, and the golden sunlight that is a near-permanent fixture makes it an incredibly seductive destination.

It is a city of passion and sophistication, the city of flamenco and Carmen and Don Juan. The Baroque architecture here (mixing the Moorish and Catholic influences) is exceptional, and Seville has the self-assurance and flair that make it a natural capital of Andalucía, and perfect for Dorne.

> "LIKE DORNISH FOOD AND DORNISH LAW, DORNISH SPEECH WAS SPICED WITH THE FLAVOURS OF THE RHOYNE, BUT A MAN COULD COMPREHEND IT."
>
> TYRION LANNISTER

In a 2012 interview, George R.R. Martin talked about the Spanish influence and how he mixed it with elements of Wales (who resisted the Norman invasion of the UK so well in the 11th century):

"Dorne is definitely influenced a bit by Spain, a bit by Wales. But nothing is one and one. I took that together. Dorne is a very special land, with a slightly different cultural basis than the rest of Westeros...it was politically apart for a long time, it was also culturally apart because of the Rhoynar and the traditions they brought, but they didn't influence the rest of Westeros so much. So the Dornish have their own particular sort of customs. I see that in Spain with the whole history, particularly the Moorish history of Spain, you know, it really sets it apart from France." (interview with Adria's News – www.adriasnews.com - October 2012)

There are myriad panoramas that would suit the recreation of the city of Dorne for GoT's fifth season, and among the general backdrop are gems such as the Royal Palace (Alcázar) and, an hour or so to the east, Osuna, home to some of the season's most dramatic scenes.

Getting there: Seville Airport has good connections to domestic Spanish and European flights. To get from the airport to the city (6 miles/10km), you can either take a taxi, which will cost around 25 euros, or look for bus services.

Stay: AlmaSevilla Hotel Palacio de Villapanes (www.palaciovillapanes.com) is a mouthful, but one of the city's best kept secrets. Eme Fusion Hotel (www.emecatedralhotel.com) will suit younger, style-conscious travellers.

See: Plaza de Espana, Seville Cathedral, Giralda, Maria Luisa Park, Metropol Parasol, Torre de Oro, Museum of Fine Arts.

Tourist Office: www.visitasevilla.es

Alcázar de Sevilla

Plaza del Triunfo, Sevilla. +34 954 502324.
www.alcazarsevilla.org

ONE OF THE COURTYARDS AT THE ALCAZAR DE
SEVILLA (IMAGE USED VIA CREATIVE COMMONS LICENSE, COURTESY OF
VISITA SEVILLA)

Welcome to the oldest European royal residence that is still
technically in use (the Spanish King and Queen will often stay
here if they're in town). The oldest parts of the palace date
back to the 12th century and has been lovingly and
flamboyantly embellished over its 1,000- year history.

The stone and wooden carvings are outstanding, as are the
colourful friezes and the intricate tiling. Within its walls, there
are some absolute treasures, from the Palacio Mudejar (which
was built by some of the same artists that worked on the
Alhambra) to the Doll's Court, the Maiden's Court and the
fabulous domed Ambassador's Room (one of the stars of GoT
Season Five).

This really is the ideal place to illustrate the Water Gardens of the Kingdom of Dorne, the Alcázar de Sevilla being transformed in to the palatial private residence of House Martell. There are several scenes with Doran Martell roaming the lush gardens and decorous private rooms, receiving Jamie Lanister, placating Ellaria Sand and generally being impressively diplomatic.

One of the early episodes of Season Five sees Doran talking to Ellaria while looking out over the Alcázar's gardens, watching his son Trystane play with his betrothed Myrcella Baratheon.

For the full GoT experience, you'll want to visit the Ambassadors' Hall, Mercury's Pool, the Baths of Maria Padilla, and the gardens.

Tip: General admission is nine Euros, but you may need to buy extra tickets for specific exhibitions. (You can check what's happening ahead of time by visiting www.alcazarsevilla.org).

Plaza de toros de Osuna

Calle Herradores, 22, Osuna. +34 955 82 00 90.

THE BULLRING IN OSUNA, AKA DAZNAK'S PIT – THE MOST EXTRAVAGANT FIGHTING PIT IN THE CITY OF MEEREEN. (PHOTO USED VIA CREATIVE COMMONS LICENSE, TAKEN BY LUKASZ LUKOMSKI)

This huge arena dates from 1904 and was designed by the architect Anibal Gonzalez – famous for building Seville's Plaza de España. The arena seats some 5,000 people.

> "AND I SAW THAT DRAGON RIPPING OFF ARMS AND LEGS, TEARING MEN IN HALF, BURNING THEM DOWN TO ASH AND BONES. PEOPLE STARTED RUNNING, TRYING TO GET OUT OF THAT PIT, BUT I COME TO SEE A SHOW, AND BY ALL OF GODS OF GHIS, I SAW ONE. I WAS UP IN THE PURPLE, SO I DIDN'T THINK THE DRAGON WAS LIKE TO TROUBLE ME." AN OLD SLAVE, TO TYRION

Given the nature of the location in GoT, it seems fitting that bullfighting still takes place here. With all the moral baggage that comes with it, it's not for us to recommend or dissuade visitors from seeing it. It certainly won't live up to the appearance of dragons, though.

Osuna's bullring, then, becomes the city of Meereen's most lavish fighting pit – Daznak's Pit. It's here that Tyrion meets Daenerys under dramatic circumstances, and where the city's rebellion against Daenerys gets off to a bloody start.

Tip: At the time of writing, tapas restaurant Casa Curro (on Plaza Salitre), was offering a GoT themed menu for fans.

Getting there: Osuna is an hour's drive east from Seville, on the A92 road. The Plaza de Toros is in the north of the town centre.

Take a GoT tour: Spain

Viator offer a half-day walking tour of Seville including the Alcázar of Seville palace that doubles as the Water Gardens of Dorne, the seat of House Martell. You can upgrade to a full-day tour that includes a coach trip to Osuna to see locations such as the old bullring that served as Danzak's Pit. More info: http://bit.ly/1G8EMl0

Game of Thrones True History

The fighting pits of meereen: The Coliseum (Rome, Italy)

Also known as the Flavian Amphitheatre, it remains the largest amphitheatre ever built, even though it dates back to the first century AD. It was famously used for gladiatorial contests – much like the Fighting Pits of Meereen – and could hold up to 80,000 spectators. It remains one of Europe's most popular tourist attractions. See also: Roman Holiday, Gladiator, The Way of the Dragon.

See it: Fly into Rome. You can purchase tickets to see the Coliseum online (www.coopculture.it). The combined ticket for the Coliseum, the Roman Forum and Palatine is valid for two days and costs €12.

The Battle of Blackwater Bay: The second Arab siege of Constantinople (Istanbul, Turkey)

This battle took place in the 8th century, as the Muslim Arabs took on the might of the Byzantine Empire. It marked the culmination of twenty years of attacks, and was a huge land and sea offensive. The siege was famed for its use of Greek Fire – a substance that is as similarly mysterious as wildfire. Its composition was a closely-guarded secret, and it burned on water with impressive effect. It was successfully employed to repel the invaders. Many historians consider the siege to be one of history's most important battles - its failure derailed the Muslim advance into south-eastern Europe for some centuries.

See it: Fly into Istanbul. Visit Istanbul Military Museum (Valikonagi Caddesi, Harbiye, +90 212 233 2720).

The Red Wedding: The Massacre of Glencoe (Glencoe, Scotland)

The 13th February 1692 remains an infamous date in Scottish history. On 2nd February, about 120 troops arrived at Glencoe under the command of Captain Robert Campbell. They were given hospitality by the MacDonalds of Glencoe as was customary in the Highlands. For the next ten days and nights the troops were given food, drink and lodgings. The MacDonalds had not sworn allegiance to the new monarch, King William, and so orders came through for the Campbells to exact punishment. Thirty eight men, women and children were killed in the massacre. The MacDonalds - killed to scare the other Highland Clans into submission - became infamous as being victims of 'murder under trust', considered even worse than normal acts of murder under the law.

Their fate reflects the bloody fate of the Starks at the Red Wedding - arranged by Lord Walder Frey as revenge against King Robb Stark for breaking the marriage pact between House Stark and House Frey. King Robb, his wife, Queen Talisa, his mother, Lady Catelyn, and most of his bannermen and men-at-arms were massacred during the marriage feast of Edmure Tully and Roslin Frey.

> "My honoured guests, be welcome within my walls and at my table. I extend to you my hospitality and protection in the light of the Seven."
>
> Lord Walder to King Robb

See it: Fly into either Edinburgh (four hours away by car) or Glasgow (two hours away by car). Visit the Glencoe Folk Museum (www.glencoemuseum.com), where you can discover more about the story of the MacDonalds and the massacre, and see a range of fascinating artefacts. Take a short walk to see the memorial monument, a stone cross on a cairn, which is dedicated to the murdered MacDonalds.

The Wall: Hadrian's Wall (Northern England)

This defensive Roman fortification was built in the second century AD during the rule of Emperor Hadrian. It originally ran between the River Tyne in the east and the Solway Firth in the west. It was originally 73 miles (117km) long, was around 16-20 feet (5-6 metres) high (the height varied).

Hadrian had apparently had 'divine instruction' to build the wall and sustain the integrity of the Roman Empire. Theories as to its real-life purpose include keeping out the marauding Scottish clans and simply as an expression of power.

Construction started in 122 AD and it took six years, with small forts being erected along the wall at a distance of every five miles (7.5km) or so. Today, some long stretches remain, and the wall was made a UNESCO World Heritage Site in 1987.

The Wall of GoT is much more impressive, but then it really has to be. The Sots – as fierce fighters as they could be – would be no match for The Wildings, let alone the army of the undead. According to the books, The Wall, patrolled so diligently by the Sworn Brothers of the Night's Watch – stood at 700 feet (230m) high and stretched 300 miles (450km) across.

"ALMOST SEVEN HUNDRED FEET HIGH IT STOOD, THREE TIMES THE HEIGHT OF THE TALLEST TOWER IN THE STRONGHOLD IT SHELTERED. HIS UNCLE SAID THE TOP WAS WIDE ENOUGH FOR A DOZEN ARMOURED KNIGHTS TO RIDE ABREAST. THE GAUNT OUTLINES OF HUGE CATAPULTS AND MONSTROUS WOODEN CRANES STOOD SENTRY UP THERE, LIKE THE SKELETONS OF GREAT BIRDS, AND AMONG THEM WALKED MEN IN BLACK AS SMALL AS ANTS." JON SNOW

George R. R. Martin talked about how the wall inspired him in an interview for the website www.smartertravel.com :

"I saw Hadrian's Wall for the first time in 1981. It was on the occasion of the first time I'd ever been to the U.K., and in fact I think the first time I'd ever left the United States. I was travelling with my friend Lisa Tuttle, who collaborated with me on the novel *Windhaven*. She had moved to the U.K. and married a British man, and she was showing me around. We were driving around the country and we reached Hadrian's Wall and it was sunset—it was at the end of the day, so all the tour buses were leaving.

We saw people getting on their buses and going away because it was just about to get dark. We really had the wall to ourselves, which I think was great because it was the fall, and it was kind of a crisp, cold day. The wind was blowing, and I climbed up on the wall and it was really just awesome.

There was nobody else around, and I stared off to the north as dusk was settling and tried to imagine what it was like to be a Roman stationed on the wall when the wall was an active protection—when it was end of the Roman world, and you didn't really know what was going to come over those hills or what was going to come out of the woods beyond that. The Romans drew men from all over this immense empire, so you might be someone from Africa or Syria or Egypt who had been assigned to this outpost. What a strange alien world it was for you.

So that was a profound experience that stayed with me. It was over a decade later when I first began *Ice and Fire*, and I still had that vision and that sense of, "I'd like to write a story about the people guarding the end of the world.""

See it: There are literally dozens of suggested routes. See www.hadrians-wall.org for more details.

Resources

The following websites have a wealth of details about the production process of GoT, including images from location shoots:

www.gameofthrones.wikia.com

www.winteriscoming.net

Made in United States
Troutdale, OR
04/12/2024